Cheapskate Living And Loving It

50 Creative Ways To Save Money, Live A Frugal Lifestyle And Enjoy Life Debt Free

Table of Contents

Introduction

I want to thank you and congratulate you for downloading the book, *"Cheapskate Living And Loving It"*.

This book contains proven steps and strategies on how to Save Money, Live a Frugal Lifestyle and Enjoy Life Debt Free.

Today many people are struggling just to make ends meet but you do not have to be one of those people! With the tips you will learn in this book, you will be living the life you always dreamed of and doing it debt free! You are going to learn not only how to save money every single day, but you are going to learn my proven strategy on how to pay off all of your bills and get out of debt.

There are tips in this book for every single person and along with the tips you will find explanations on how to follow through, as well as how much money you will be able to save each year by following these tips. If you choose to implement just a few of the tips in this book, you will find yourself saving hundreds of dollars each year that you can put toward getting out of debt and staying debt free!

The frugal lifestyle is a great one, so don't feel like you are going to have to do without the things you love just to save money. I am going to show you how to enjoy all of the things you do right now but save as much money as you can in the process!

Thanks again for downloading this book, I hope you enjoy it!

Chapter 1

Saving Money on Your Grocery Bill

Groceries are one of the largest bills that many of us have to budget for each month. It is not a luxury item that we can choose to live without, but there are tons of ways for you to save on your grocery bill each week!

1. Start clipping coupons. Every year companies send out millions of dollars worth of coupons, but only a fraction of them are used. If you take just one hour each week and start clipping coupons, you will find that you will be able to buy name brand foods for much cheaper than you would pay for even the store brands. At first, this is going to cost you a few dollars per week but in the long run it is going to pay off substantially.

    Now, I want to explain that along with our food we usually buy our household supplies as well as our toiletries, so that is going to be part of what you will save money on with coupons.

    The first thing you are going to do is to collect your coupons. You can print these offline or clip them out of your Sunday paper. There are even sites online where you can purchase inserts for as low as 25 cents each plus shipping. This makes it a lot cheaper than buying a Sunday paper, which usually runs about $2.50 on average.

    If you have a large family to feed, you will be able to purchase multiple inserts to save you a ton of money. Now, many people will clip a few coupons and go out to the local store and use them right away. You are not going to do this. You are going to save your coupons for when there is a sale and stock up on that item for free or almost free.

You need to stock up enough of that item to get you through about 6 weeks, which is when the item will go on sale again. Here is an example that is using hygiene products, there was a specific brand name shampoo and conditioner that was on sale at my local store. The normal price was $3.50 per bottle but it was on sale for $2.50 a bottle.

I knew I had ten $5 off two bottle coupons, so I ended up getting 10 shampoos and 10 conditioners absolutely free. Another one that I just took advantage of was a very expensive lotion that was on sale at my store for $3.00 per bottle. I had ten $5 off two coupons which made them 50 cents a piece, but to top that off I had a coupon that gave me $5 off a purchase of $25 or more making 20 lotions absolutely free!

You can do this on food just like you can on body products, cleaning products, and laundry supplies. Wait for a sale, top it with a coupon and get the lowest price possible!

2. Grocery shop at your local dollar store. I am talking about your dollar store that sells everything for a dollar! They sell groceries there too. They also take coupons, which makes everything very cheap. For example, they sell cereal at my local dollar store. Cereal for a dollar is great, but throw a coupon on top of that and get it for 66 cents a box, now that is amazing!

3. Plan your meals each week and use your grocery store flyer to do so! Every week you should get your grocery store flyer in the mail, use this along with your coupons to decide what you are going to eat for the week. Write down all the ingredients you will need for you meals planning them around what is on sale.

4. Shop in your own pantry. This is a big one! So many times people do not realize what they actually have in their cabinets. Have you ever went to the store, saw

something you thought you needed, bought it only to come home and find 3 of the exact same untouched product in your cabinet? Once you have created your list of all the ingredients you will need for the week, check your pantry to see if you have any of them already in there.

5. Cook once, eat three times. This is one of my favorites. Did you know that you could actually get three meals for a family of four out of just one chicken? This is how I do it; first, I boil the cut up chicken to make chicken and dumplings with. I remove all the meat from the bones after the chicken has boiled; use the stock to make my dumplings adding about 1/3 of the meat. Then, I put the bones and skin in the crock-pot to make chicken noodle soup stock. Finally, I am able to throw some barbeque sauce on the 2/3 chicken meat I have left and serve barbequed chicken sandwiches.

   You can do this with tons of different foods and cut back on what you are paying for meat each week!

6. Find a local discount grocery store. Many people like to say that the food you are buying at a discount grocery store is no good and you will get sick if you eat it. That in fact is not true. Each week I load up my children and drive 50 miles to the closest discount grocery store. The reason is that I am able to literally triple my money I have budgeted for groceries. For example, I am able to buy whole frozen organic chickens for no more than $3. Now I have told you how we can make one chicken last three days, so it is costing me $1 a day for our chicken!

   You can purchase everything you need at a discount grocery store! They sell milk way cheaper than you will ever find at the grocery store and it is not out of date. They sell a 24 case of yogurt for 2 bucks! Check around and see if you have a discount grocery store near you, even if you have to drive a little ways, it is worth it because you will be saving more than you can imagine on your grocery bill.

7. So many times, we have leftovers after dinner and think nothing about throwing them in the trash. If you really want to save money, you need to rethink leftovers. Make them into something different, take them for lunch the next day look at those leftovers as your money, don't throw your money away. There are even times I purposely make leftovers because I know we can eat it on another night or I plan to make it into something else. Another great thing my kids love to do is leftover day. We save what is leftover throughout the week, throw it in the freezer, then on Sunday have a buffet type meal with all types of choices. This ensures nothing goes to waste.

8. Stop snacking or allowing children to graze while they are at home. So much food can disappear if you allow your children to get in the pantry and eat whenever they feel like it. You need to set up a schedule because the fact is that children as well as many adults will eat simply because the food is there and they can.

9. Set a budget and stick to it. If you set a budget and stick to it you will learn very quickly how to stretch you money. I am not joking when I say stick to it. If you go shopping on Saturdays and run out of food on Thursday, you will learn how to stretch whatever is left in your cabinets and you will be much more cautious the next week.

10. Only go to the store once a week and go with a list. Never go in the store without a list of the items you intend to buy. If you do, you will find that you are over spending and not getting the food that you really need to prepare meals with. Take your list and don't allow temptation to overtake you. Never go to the store just to pick up one or two things once you have already done

your weekly shopping. So many times, we go in looking for one or two items and come out with a cartload. If you forget something, make due or figure something else out, but do not go back into that store. If you absolutely have to go in, only take the amount of money needed to purchase the item you need. Leave the debit card in the car and grab a little cash.

Chapter 2

Saving Money on Your Electric Bill

Oh how we dread seeing that electric bill each and every month. There used to be times that I had no idea how much electricity I had used and felt completely helpless. That was until I received an electric bill that was more than my house payment last winter. I decided things had to change. Here are some changes you can make.

1. No more dryer! Did you know that you could lower your electric bill tremendously if you just stop using your dryer? In the spring, summer and most of the fall you can line dry your clothes outside. In the winter, you can purchase a cheap (usually around $5) drying rack for your house. These racks usually hold about one load of laundry each.

2. How many times have we been told that we should turn the heat down in our homes if we want to lower our electric bill? I was taught that you should turn it down, then if you get really cold, warm up the house and turn it back down again. Then a study came out by my local electric company that said do not set your thermostat at one temperature and leave it there unless you are going to be out of the house for several hours or are going to bed. What you can do is in the winter start with your thermostat at 68 degrees, if you are comfortable at that temperature drop it to 67. Continue to do this until you find the temperature that you just cannot stand. In my house, we often have jackets, multiple layers or blankets on us in the wintertime.

   In the summer, you want to do the opposite. Set your thermostat at 74 degrees and see how warm you can stand it. On the days that it is not extremely hot, open your windows, turn on the fans and let the summer air in your home. Most of the time during the spring and fall you should allow your windows to be open since the temperature outside is not too hot or too cold.

3. Check all of your windows and doors for gaps as well as around your baseboards if you have a basement. In older homes, this is where a lot of heat is lost and cold air comes in at. If you find gaps, fix them.

4. Close off the rooms that are not in use. Shut the doors to the rooms that no one is in. If the kids are in the living room, there is no reason to heat the bedrooms. If no one is in the bathroom, shut that door. This will keep the majority of the heat in the main part of the house near the thermostat, which will ensure your furnace is not over working and you are not wasting any heat. You can do the same thing in the summer!

5. Open your curtains in the winter and close them in the summer! Find the windows in your home that face the sun, when the sun is high in the sky, open those curtains in the winter, this will help heat your house. In the summer, it will heat your house as well so make sure you close the curtains.

6. Unplug everything! Did you know that while you sleep at night and all of your electronics are shut off, they are still using electricity? Even that cell phone charger you leave plugged into the wall when your phone is not charging is constantly using electricity. When you finish using something, unplug it.

7. Wash your clothes in cold water. This will work for the majority of people, unless you have an extremely dirty job you should wash all of your clothes in cold water. If you have clothes that are very soiled, you should keep them separate from the rest of your clothing and wash them in hot water by themselves. You should also make sure to wash your whites in hot water at least once per month to ensure they stay bright white.

8. Remove some of the light bulbs! In my house, I have two chandeliers that hang from the ceiling, each of these takes eight light bulbs. In no way do we need eight light bulbs to light our rooms, so I only put two light bulbs in each one. True it does not have the same effect as all eight, but you will save money if you don't fill up your light fixtures.

9. Change your filters in your furnace/air conditioner every month to keep it from over working and to keep the air flowing.

10. If you have the choice between the microwave oven and your conventional oven, use the microwave, it uses 90 percent less electricity than the conventional oven. If you have to use the conventional oven open it up after you shut if off in the winter, you can use that heat that is trapped in there to warm your house.

Chapter 3

Television, Phone, Internet, Cells and More

I once found myself paying over $100 for my satellite bill, $70 for my internet, $60 for a home phone and over $100 a month for my cell phone. I was tired of wasting money on these things, so I made a few changes. Here are a few tips for you for saving money on these bills and more!

1. Cut out the satellite. There is no reason for you to pay that huge satellite bill each month, instead opt for Netflix or something like Netflix. Today there are tons of different programs you can choose from and they start at about $7 a month. Sure, you will be one season behind on the shows you watch, but really what does that matter when you are saving over $1,000 a year!

   Instead of using the video on demand service, wait and watch the movie later. There is no point in paying $5 to watch a movie once, when you can purchase it at a resale shop for $1 in just a few months and watch it whenever you want. Or just order it from Netflix. You can have your movie in the mail in just a few days!

2. The phone bill was also another huge issue for me as well as my internet bill. Now, of course you can cut these bills completely if you really do not need them, but I have to have them for my work. I went to my local phone company and talked to them about the price. I ended up being able to pay just $69 each month for both services instead of the $130 I was paying. If you don't need the internet for work or school, it is best to go ahead and have it and your home phone shut off and use only your cell phone for these services.

3. Speaking of cell phones, we can really run up a huge bill each month. The way I got rid of this bill was at my local Wal-Mart. Yes you heard me right. I went to Wal-Mart, picked up a $10 prepaid phone and started looking at plans. I do not need the internet on my phone since I have it at home, so I am able to pay $35 per month for unlimited talk and text. Now, if I needed the internet on my phone and did not have it at home, I could pay $50 per month for unlimited talk text and web. This is a huge savings over any contract you will get with a cell phone. The phones are just as good as the ones you get with a contract and you don't have to be stuck with some out of date flip phone. If you are looking to save money on your cell phone bill, check out the prepaid cell phones available in your area.

4. Consider working from home. This is a huge money saver. Before I worked from home, I had to pay a babysitter to watch my three children, I had to pay for gas to get back and forth to work and the list went on and on. Now my children stay at home with me while I work in my office, saving me over $1,200 a month plus gas and so on. Figure out if it is feasible for you to work at home and determine how much money you will save if you do.

5. Stop purchasing items you have to make payments on. If you are going to purchase a car, make sure you have the cash to do so. The last car I purchased after searching for several hours online cost me $500. I sold my other car for $500 and paid cash for the one I own now. The car is not beat up or a rust bucket, it is a 94 Lincoln that runs like a charm. If you take the time to search for these deals, you are going to save a ton in interest in the long run.

6. Buy used and save the difference. Going along with not making payments on anything, stop buying everything brand new. Find used items and save your money. Six

years ago I purchased a used washer and dryer. I am very picky about my clothes, so after 2 hours of scrubbing them out, I was ready to use them. I paid $50 total for both and they are currently in my laundry room doing a perfect job. Granted, I do not use the dryer often, but it is there when I need it. You can do this with all of your appliances, but you need to make sure you are getting a good deal. For example, I went to buy a used deep freeze. It cost $100, so I decided I wanted to compare prices with a new one and found I could get a larger one that was on sale at a local store new for $60. Don't assume just because it is being sold as used that you are getting the lowest price you can.

7. Cut up the credit cards and pay them off. I personally have never owned a credit card and I never want to. I watched my parents have to file bankruptcy due to overspending on credit cards. If you currently own a credit card, cut it up, call the company and see if they will lower your interest rate then start paying them off. Once they are paid off, do not apply for new ones. Live on what cash you have in your pocket and do not accumulate debt.

8. Consider quitting smoking and drinking. The average smoker spends over $150 each month on cigarettes and depending on how much you are drinking you could be spending upwards of $100 on that as well. That is $3,000 a year that you can put toward something more important. Saving money and being frugal has a lot to do with being healthy as well and just imagine the amount of money you will end up saving on future doctor bills if you quit now.

9. Shop at thrift shops and yard sales. You may think that you will not find anything that you like if you purchase from thrift shops or yard sales, but the truth is you can find amazing treasures. For example, my entire living room is furnished with Ashley furniture. I bought it at a

yard sale from an elderly couple. It was very well cared for and I spent a total of $200 for a couch, loveseat, and two chairs. All of the pictures in my home have come from thrift shops, as well as all of the televisions I own. You can purchase a 40-inch television from a thrift shop for about $40. This is because they usually do not have the remote with them, but guess what; you can order a universal remote from Amazon for about $10. So you end up spending around $50 for the entire thing!

10. Find things to do that do not cost any money. Often times people get bored and they decide that they want to go spend some money to entertain themselves, instead find things to do that are free. Such as a hike in the woods, visiting your local park, taking your kids swimming in the river or teaching them about volunteering at the local animal shelter. You can also watch your local paper for free events that are being held in your town such as parades, car shows or cook offs.

Chapter 4

And There is More!

There are even more ways for you to save money each and every day! I know at this point you may be getting a little overwhelmed, but choose a few money saving ideas from this book and implement them. Once you are able to do them with consistency add a few more. This is not all or nothing here. Remember, saving just a little will help you become encouraged to save even more!

1. Take advantage of end of season sales. Did you know that you can get brand name clothes brand new for literally pennies on the dollar? At the end of each season clothing goes on sale, if you watch the prices you will be able to get $100 shirts for a couple bucks! When you have growing kids this is a great way to keep them in stylish clothing without breaking the bank. What I do is purchase one or two sizes bigger than what my child is currently wearing so that the new clothes will fit when that season comes around again. You can also do this for holiday decorations, costumes, and even purchase your Christmas presents for the next year right after this years Christmas! You will end up saving about 90% on Christmas and you will be prepared for the following year!

2. Cook all of your meals at home. If you find that you are going out to eat more than once a month, you really need to think about cooking more meals at home. You see, for what you spend on one meal at a fast food place, you could make dinner for four at home and it's going to be much more healthy.

3. If something is broken, do not throw it away, fix it! We live in a society where everything is disposable, but if

you really want to save money, learn how to fix the things that are broken.

4. Rent instead of own. There are those who will disagree with this, but if you rent a house instead of purchase it, you don't have to pay home owners insurance, you don't have to worry about how you will pay for a new water heater, just call the landlord and let them deal with it.

5. Move to a smaller cheaper house. This is one that gets a lot of people. We want our children to have their own bedrooms, to have a huge house to live in and we want others to think we are well off. If you are paying for more house than you really need, you are wasting your money. I had to consider this when I was living in a five bedroom house realizing we actually only used a few of the rooms. So much space was not being used, therefore so much of my money was being wasted. Look into a smaller cheaper house if you find that all of your house is not being used.

6. Plant a garden. Gardening is very inexpensive and it can produce lots of great food for you to eat. You can also sell the excess at your local farmers market in order to make some extra cash on the side!

7. Raise your own chickens. Many people have trouble eating the chickens that they raise, so for those people, just get enough chickens to produce the number of eggs you need each day! If you have extra sell them. In the summer, you can allow your chickens to roam your yard and eat up all the bugs along with some grass to cut back on chicken feed.

8. Learn how to cut your own hair or at least your children's hair. In our house, I cut everyone's hair except my own. I have very long hair and when I want it trimmed I am willing to pay the $8 to have it done, but

only once or twice a year. If you can cut your own hair that is great, if not find a low priced salon and have them do it on the cheap.

9. Dying your own hair can also save you a ton of money. With salon prices sky rocketing, you can save about $100 each time you dye your hair at home depending on how long it is.

10. Take snacks with you wherever you go. How often do you jump in the car to go somewhere and the kids start complaining that they are hungry? You end up stopping by a fast food joint and spending $40 on junk food. Instead, grab some Ziploc bags and stuff them full of healthy snacks. The next time the kids say they are, hungry hand them a bag and be on your way.

Chapter 5

Final Tips for You to Save Money!

In this next chapter, I am going to give you ten more tips to help you save money. Here are ten more tips to help save you money every day!

1. Find out if your bank is charging you fees. What happens if your bank account gets overdrawn by accident? How much do you end up paying? If you find that you are paying fees at your bank, find a bank that works for you. For example, my bank offers a plan for free that allows you to overdraw by $600 as long as you pay off the balance within a month. This is great in case there is some type of emergency and you don't have to worry about paying $30 a day in overdraft fees!

2. Have your bills automatically taken out of your bank account each month. Life is fast and sometimes we forget to send that bill or jump online to pay it, so instead of getting charged late fees each month, just sign up to auto pay your bills each month. This can save a few hundred dollars in late fees each year.

3. Sell the things you don't need! Don't give away the clothes that your children have out grown, take them to a thrift shop and sell them on consignment or better yet have a yard sale and make some extra cash. I always send everything to the thrift shop because I don't have much time to plan a yard sale and they do all the work for me. You do need to understand they will take a percentage of what your stuff sells for though.

4. Stop buying paper towels (unless of course you have a coupon that makes them free). Instead of buying paper

towels, go buy a pack of white wash cloths for $3 that you will use specifically for cleaning.

5. Freeze the items you buy in bulk. A few weeks ago I went to the local discount grocery store and they had Coffee Mate creamer on sale for 2 for a dollar. This stuff is very expensive, so I purchased several. I knew that if I did not use them quickly they would go bad, so instead, I put them in the freezer and each week I can grab one out to use. I now have enough creamer for several months and saved around $80! You can freeze tons of items you find on sale like this, and if you don't know ask someone who works at the store, they can usually tell you.

6. If you are going to run your appliances (dishwasher, washing machine, dryer) run them at night. The off peak hour prices for electricity are cheaper than during the day!

7. Save all of your change for a year. Each time you empty your pockets or your purse, put your loose change in a jar, at the end of the year deposit this change into a savings account.

8. Do you get a tax return? Many people with children get a tax return each year, many of these people also end up wasting this money on items they do not really need. Instead of wasting your tax return, create a plan to use it to pay up your bills for several months in advance, or use it to pay down some of that debt. This is a great chance for you to benefit yourself in the days to come.

9. Use a thirty-day plan. If you are in the store and you see something that you want, put it back on the shelf and wait for thirty days. If in thirty days you still want the item, see if you can fit it into your budget, but chances are you are going to forget about the item because you only wanted it on impulse.

10. Need it or want it. Many people have to realize there is a difference between need and want. They go into the store see an item they want and tell themselves they need it for this specific reason. A need is something that you will not be able to live without. A want is obviously something you can live without but would really like. Ask yourself if you really need the item before buying it.

Chapter 6

How to Get Out of Debt for Good

Throughout this book, I have given you tips on how to save money, but what are you supposed to do with the money you are saving? Of course you can put it in the bank in a savings account, but before you do that you want to get yourself out of debt.

It does not matter what kind of debt you have, the technique I am going to teach you will get you completely out of debt in the shortest amount of time possible.

First, I want you to get a pen and paper and start writing down all of the debt you own and how much you currently own on that debt. Like this:

Medical $6,543

MasterCard $4,154

Visa $2,894

Car $7,325

And so on. Now once you have your list, you are going to find the debt that you owe the least amount on. Using the above example, you would want to begin with the Visa card. If your minimum monthly payment is $200, I want you to budget that $200 into your monthly bills. I also want you to add an extra $50 to $100 onto the payment depending on how much you can afford.

Keep making your minimum payments on the rest of your bills until the Visa is paid in full. Next, you would move on to the MasterCard. Let's say you have been paying $300 a month toward that debt, I want you to take that $300 plus the $200 you were paying for your Visa as well as the $50 to $100 dollars you added on to the minimum payment and pay that all towards your MasterCard. This would make your payment $550 to $600 dollars a month.

After you have paid off your MasterCard, you are going to move on to the next bill. In this example you would begin paying off your medical bills. So, if you are paying a minimum of $100 dollars per month toward your medical bills, you are going to take the $200 you were paying toward your Visa before it was paid off, plus the $50 to $100 extra you were sending in, add to that the $300 you were paying toward your MasterCard before it was paid off, and you will be sending $650-$700 dollars per month toward your medical bills.

You will continue this process until all of your debt is paid off. Then, you will keep following the tips I have given you in this book to ensure you do not accrue more debt. It is important that you take the money you were paying toward previous bills and budget it for the next bill, because otherwise you are going to find yourself spending and wasting all of that money that should be going to bills. Once your debt is paid off, you need to set it up with your bank so the money is deposited directly into a savings account each and every month.

Doing this will ensure that you are not wasting your money, but setting up a nice nest egg for yourself and your family.

This process is simple, but depending on the amount of debt, you have it can take some time. Remember the tip I gave you about your tax return, if you do get one, you can also use this to pay down these debts making the process go much, much faster.

Chapter 7

Frugal Lifestyle

Living frugally and without debt is a lifestyle and it may take some time for you to get used to it, but it is so freeing that it is worth all of the work that goes into it. When you decide that you want to live frugally and without debt, sit down and make a list of reasons why you want to do so.

Keep this list of reasons close by so that if you start to feel like you are missing out on certain things in life you will be reminded of what your goals are. One of the rules in our house is that if we don't have a coupon for it, we do not purchase it. So, if you really are wanting something search the internet for a coupon for it or just wait until it goes on sale.

Another part of living the frugal lifestyle is taking care of the things you have and respecting what you have spent your money on. So what if you own a $50 couch, that is $50 out of your pocket, take care of it and respect it.

Finally, I want to talk to you about passing on the frugal lifestyle. How great would it feel if you could say your children would never be in debt? What about if you knew that they would never go without or want because you taught them how to save and spend money wisely. If for no other reason than this, I hope that you take the tips in this book and implement them into your life.

You must understand before you decide to make these changes, that living frugally and saving money does take some extra work in life! It does take giving up some conveniences, but trust me if you follow through with this in a few months you won't even miss them.

Now, how are you going to implement these changes? As I mentioned before, I want you to pick a few of the tips I have given you and start making those changes in your life. Once you have applied these changes, after a few weeks add a few more changes.

You don't want to make too many changes at once because if you do you will find that they are harder to stick to. Most people want to make huge changes in their lives and they fail because they really are asking too much of themselves. But if you add in small changes, you will barely notice them and you will raise your chances of being successful.

One thing that you are going to do while you are making these changes is fail. You are going to see something in the store that you really like and buy it on impulse or order something off of the internet, but when this happens don't give up, keep your head up and start again.

We as humans only learn through failure and if you fail along the way, take note of it then move on. This only gets easier as time goes on.

Conclusion

Thank you again for downloading this book!

I hope this book was able to help you to save money, get out of debt and live a more frugal life!

The next step is to get started using these tips and paying off that debt!

Finally, if you enjoyed this book, then I'd like to ask you for a favor, would you be kind enough to leave a review for this book on Amazon? It'd be greatly appreciated!

Click here to leave a review for this book on Amazon!

Thank you and good luck!

Check Out My Other Books

Below you'll find some of my other popular books that are popular on Amazon and Kindle as well. Simply click on the links below to check them out. Alternatively, you can visit my author page on Amazon to see other work done by me.

http://www.amazon.com/Living-Frugal-Loving-Creative-Simple-ebook/dp/B00Q7MVGEE

http://www.amazon.com/Minimalism-Made-Easy-Declutter-Happiness-ebook/dp/B00P38D074

http://www.amazon.com/How-Declutter-Simplify-Your-Life-ebook/dp/B00NUGACJK

http://www.amazon.com/DIY-Cleaning-Made-Easy-Declutter-ebook/dp/B00PDWNKDE

http://www.amazon.com/DIY-Household-Hacks-Beginners-Organized-ebook/dp/B00Q7X23TU

Made in the USA
Monee, IL
16 March 2021